SCENTED GERANIUMS

KNOWING, GROWING, AND ENJOYING SCENTED PELARGONIUMS

JIM BECKER & FAYE BRAWNER

INTERWEAVE PRESS

Scented Geraniums
by Jim Becker and Faye Brawner

Design and Production, Karen M. Gogela
Illustrations, Susan Strawn
Text ©1996, Jim Becker and Faye Brawner

 INTERWEAVE PRESS
201 East Fourth Street
Loveland, Colorado 80537
USA

printed in Hong Kong by Sing Cheong

Becker, Jim
    Scented geraniums: knowing, growing, and enjoying
pelargoniums/by Jim Becker and Faye Brawner.
        p.   cm.
    Includes index.
    ISBN 1-883010-18-7
    1. Scented geraniums.   I. Brawner, Faye.   II. Title.
SB303.S34B435 1996
635.9'33216—dc20   96-43368
                                                    CIP
                                                    95 433 68

First printing:IWP—10M:296:CC

Scented Geraniums

KNOWING,
GROWING,
AND ENJOYING
SCENTED
PELARGONIUMS

TABLE OF CONTENTS

INTRODUCTION

When our editor first read the book, she asked gingerly, "Are scented pelargoniums really as fussy and fragile as all this? Why would anyone bother?" This surprised us greatly. Had we presented such an ominous list of do's and don'ts, of lurking pests and diseases, of potential pitfalls that readers would give up before beginning?

Before you read another word of this book, read this one—relax! Gardeners who grow scenteds know that most varieties are pretty tough, although there are a couple of fussy exceptions. They will survive in less than optimum conditions. The goal, of course, is not mere survival. Survival is a word best left for botanists and ecologists who peer at the edge of existence. Gardeners want their plants to thrive, and that is what this book is all about. We hope our list of do's and don'ts anticipates your questions and will help prevent potential pitfalls.

Don't worry if your thermometer reads a few degrees higher than our stated ideal growing temperature for scenteds. Your plants won't croak. Honest. If temperatures are soaring, provide your plants with shade protection. That's what gardening is all about. Be confident, have fun, follow our hard-earned advice and your plants will thrive. We hope you'll come to love scenteds as much as we do.

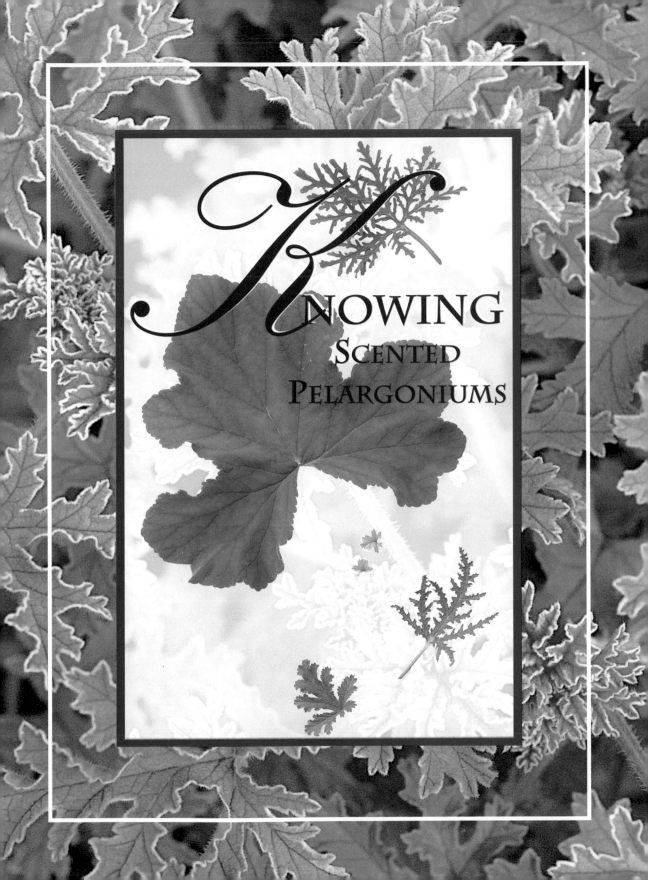

Knowing Scented Pelargoniums

Scenteds are a delight in the garden, whether grown in containers or in the ground.
Photograph by Michael Vassar.

A Plant FOR ALL Seasons

TO KNOW SCENTED GERANIUMS is to appreciate an olfactory pleasure unlike any other offered by nature. The fragrant wonder of scenteds is ingeniously hidden in their leaves. Simply pinch the foliage of these easy-to-grow plants and you will be greeted with the luscious scent of mint, rose, fruit, nuts, or more.

These aromatic jewels attract the eye as well as the nose by their myriad interesting shapes, textures, and colors, and they flower intermittently throughout the growing season. Unlike those of many of the common garden varieties, the blooms of scenteds don't overshadow the beauty of their leaves, but rather emphasize it with soft contrast.

Scenteds are a delight in the garden, whether grown in the ground or in containers. But the joy of these plants is that they can be brought inside, where you can take pleasure in them throughout the year—they are living potpourri for the home.

Overwintering scenteds indoors allows year-round enjoyment.
Photograph by Joe Coca.

What's IN A Name?

THE RULES OF NOMENCLATURE (not to mention common sense) dictate that each plant can have only one true name and that no two plants can have the same name. The universal language used since the Middle Ages to designate these names is Latin, but the system of binomial ("two-name") nomenclature in use today dates to Linnaeus's work in the eighteenth century.

Each type of naturally occurring plant which botanists deem to be different from all others is called a species. Each has its own two-part Latin name, or binomial. For example, the species of scented geranium commonly called 'Old-Fashioned Rose' is named *Pelargonium graveolens*. The first part of the binomial, which is capitalized and italicized, is the generic name. It is shared by a whole group of closely related plants, which together make up a genus.

Plants within a genus are differentiated from one another by the second part of the binomial, which is the specific epithet. There are more than 250 members of the genus *Pelargonium*, but there is only one *P. graveolens*. (The generic name of a binomial is abbreviated after the first mention unless an abbreviation would be ambiguous.) The specific epithet, which is italicized but not capitalized, is often an adjective that describes some feature of the plant. It may be used as part of the binomial of several different plants as long as they are not in the same genus. *Graveolens*, which means "heavily scented", is also the specific epithet for the herbs rue (*Ruta graveolens*) and dill (*Anethum graveolens*). An epithet may also refer to the person for whom a plant is named or the location where it is found. The Bibliography lists several books that give translations of Latin names; these are both informative and enjoyable reading.

The plants commonly called scented geraniums in the United States, like the common garden geranium, actually belong to the genus

Pelargonium, not, as might be supposed, to the genus *Geranium.* Recently, plant societies in the United States and abroad have been making a concerted effort to adopt the word "pelargonium" for the common as well as the generic name of these delightful plants. In keeping with their work, and contrary to the title of this book, we will from hereon also refer to them as scented pelargoniums, and not scented geraniums. Note that when "pelargonium" is used as a common name, it is neither capitalized nor italicized.

Only a few scented pelargoniums are natural species, known by their well-known common names as well as their Latin binomials. Most of the scenteds are the result of hybridization between species or other hybrids. (See hybridization, page 59.) Of the dozens of offspring resulting from such crosses, only the best ones have been selected, and each of these selections, called a cultivar (cultivated variety), is given a unique proper name. Cultivar names such as 'Snowflake' are not usually in Latin, and are set within single quotation marks and not italicized. Because all of the cultivars listed in this book belong to the genus *Pelargonium,* we've omitted the generic name when referring to cultivar names.

'Old-Fashioned Rose' *(Pelargonium graveolens)*
Photograph by Michael Vassar

BOTANY

THERE ARE SOME 250 naturally occurring species of *Pelargonium*, most native to South Africa. Many have highly scented leaves, which are thought to be a natural deterrent against grazing animals, but only a few are the scented pelargoniums used in gardens. The ease of hybridization, both by man and especially the chance efforts of insects, has led to countless cultivars being offered by nurseries, but only a few of these are true species. Among the best known are 'Apple' (*P. odoratissiumm*), 'Coconut' (*P. grossularioides*), 'Lemon' (*P. crispum*), 'Old - Fashioned Rose' (*P. graveolens*), and 'Peppermint' (*P. tomentosum*).

Lady Plymouth and Peppermint grouped with annuals and perennials in Lucy Hardiman's garden, Portland, Oregon. **Photograph by Jim Becker.**

The scent of scented pelargoniums is contained in small beads of oil produced in glands at the base of tiny leaf hairs. Bruising or crushing the leaf breaks the beads and releases their fragrance. A few varieties need but a casual brushing to produce a noticeable fragrance.

Some scented pelargoniums have an easily recognizable fragrance such as lemon or peppermint, whereas others may smell like cinnamon to one person and citrus to someone else.

The leaves of scented pelargoniums vary not only in their fragrances, but also in their shapes, sizes, colors, and textures. They range in length from 1/2 inch (1 cm) to more than 6 inches (15 cm). Some are almost circular; others are lobed to varying degrees; still others are as finely divided as a fern. The most common leaf color is medium green, but leaves may also be deeper green or even grayish or silver in tone. Some leaves are splashed or edged with white, cream, or yellow. Purplish brown may blotch leaf centers or color their veins and midribs. Leaf textures can be smooth or rough, and raspy, hairy, or soft and velvety.

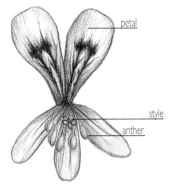

Scented pelargoniums vary widely in their overall appearance, but their flowers have several characteristics in common. The flowers are grouped in clusters, called umbels, of from two to fifty individual flowers (florets); most scented varieties have between five and ten. The florets are usually five-parted: there are five sepals, ten stamens (of which two to seven bear anthers), and five carpels. The carpels and their styles are joined, and the fancied resemblance of the long, narrow seed capsule to a stork's bill gives rise to the old common name, storksbill, as well as to the generic name *Pelargonium*, which is derived from the Greek word *pelargos*, meaning "stork".

Although scented pelargoniums are grown mainly for their fragrant foliage, the flowers are attractive as well. Most have five petals and are called single-flowered. There are a few hybrids that have eight to ten petals, and these are known as double-flowered cultivars. The petals range in size from a scant 1/8 inch (3 mm) up to 1 inch (2 cm) long; they are most commonly white, rose, or lavender, less commonly salmon or red. The most vivid colors among scenteds are found in cultivars derived from crosses with other types of pelargoniums, such as the hybrid group known as regals. The petals of the single-flowered scenteds are grouped with two at the top and three at the bottom. The upper petals are usually wider and are often stippled with deep purple or reddish markings. *Pelargonium*, along with four other genera, belong to the Geranium family (Geraniaceae). Species and cultivars of *Erodium* and *Geranium* are grown in rock gardens and perennial borders. The presence of a small nectar tube that extends down the stalk of the floret from the base of one of the sepals distinguishes *Pelargonium* from the other genera in the family. The opening of the tube is difficult to see on the surface of the stalk unless you remove the petals and look straight down at the cup of sepals.

In their native South Africa, scented pelargoniums are perennial, living and flowering for several years. The species vary in habit from low, scrambling trailers to shrubs more than 7 feet (2 m) high, and they are found in a multitude of habitats from the forest understory to the seashore. Though most of these areas have fast-draining soils and seasonal rainfall, the scenteds are not, as has been claimed, desert dwellers. Some succulent *Pelargonium* species are adapted to desert conditions, but the scenteds are not among them.

Scented Pelargoniums
in the Landscape

A GARDEN IS A WONDROUS, intricate tapestry. We can step back and admire the total image, but we also find great pleasure in exploring the smaller secrets held in its elemental fragrances, shapes, colors, and textures. A garden is especially fascinating and sometimes frustrating because, unlike a wild wood or meadow, it is our own creation. If we take our role of creator seriously, as many gardeners do, we never rest, but are always searching for something new and special to add to its design.

Scented pelargoniums can add wonder to any garden. Unlike most garden plants, their fragrances come not from transitory blossoms, but may be summoned from the leaves (or appreciated in potpourris, cosmetics, and bouquets) any day of the year.

Scented pelargoniums can be grown as outdoor perennials in North America only in frost-free regions. In cooler climates, they may be grown as annual bedding plants. They are a welcome alternative to pansies, petunias, marigolds, and zinnias. Some varieties can thrive in poor, dry soil where other

An underplanting of various scented pelargoniums at Barn Owl Nursery, Wilsonville, Oregon. Blooming varieties, from left to right: Brunswick, Mrs. Taylor, Paton's Unique, and Strawberry. Photograph by Jim Becker.

Pots of Nutmeg (foreground), Lilian Pottinger (left rear), and Peacock. Photograph by Jim Becker.

A pot of Old-Fashioned Rose hides the downspout in the corner of this deck. Photograph by Jim Becker.

annuals would not succeed.

Scenteds can be massed in beds. Low growing types, like the gray-leaved 'Nutmeg', make excellent edgings for pathways and walks. Clumps of different scenteds, planted close to steps and gateways where one can't help brushing them in passing, are a great way to make an entrance more memorable. Large, shrubby cultivars such as 'Old-Fashioned Rose' are just the thing to perk up otherwise mundane parts of the garden. Planted at the ends of vegetable rows, they will offer a refreshing scent as well as a bountiful harvest of leaves for potpourri.

Scented pelargoniums are especially nice when intermingled with perennials or other annuals. For instance, the soft, broad green leaves of 'Peppermint' (*P. tomentosum*) are an excellent foil for the shell pink flowers of a dianthus or flowering tobacco (*Nicotiana* sp.), the finely divided foliage of 'Pungent Peppermint' sets off the circular leaves of nasturtiums, and the greenery of 'Old-Fashioned Rose' fills in the bareness at the base of a hybrid tea rose.

As effective as they are when grown in the ground, scented pelargoniums often have their finest moments in containers. Pots and pelargoniums seem made for each other. Containers offer many advantages in a landscape, chief of which is their portability. You can put them anywhere that you can carry them and care for them, and when you tire of the way they look, you can rearrange them. Portable pots let you highlight different potted plants at different times of the year if you like.

A row of large potted pelargoniums can serve as a low barrier, confining and enclosing a space like a small wall or hedge. Pots can be used for spot color around the garden; larger ones are useful for hiding hoses, electrical boxes, and other eyesores. Scenteds in pots can define the edges of patios and walkways, help in locating and negotiating outdoor stairways, or highlight architectural details such as windows, doorways, and arches. They can invite you down a pathway and through a garden gate. They also complement garden ornaments such as fountains, sundials, and statuary. Scented pelargoniums can enhance any deck, patio, or gazebo; place them so that their foliage is within easy reach of chairs and benches for maximum enjoyment.

We like to make mini-gardens of four or five different scented pelargoniums in half barrels. We might place a tall, upright type such as 'Mabel Grey', 'Lime', or *P. crispum* 'Major' at the back of the planter with a medium-sized, bushy variety such as 'Fair Ellen' or 'Concolor Lace' in the center and shorter, trailing kinds such as 'Nutmeg', 'Apple', or 'Dean's Delight' in the foreground.

Clockwise from rear (window): Charity, Mabel Grey, Dean's Delight, and Nutmeg. Photograph by Jim Becker.

Many varieties are suitable for hanging baskets or window boxes. Sprawling forms of 'Coconut', 'Apple', 'Lilian Pottinger', 'Old Spice', 'Nutmeg', or *P. crispum* 'Minor' may be mixed with trailing annuals such as verbenas or portulacas, or with perennial herbs such as creeping thymes for a fuller effect.

Although scented pelargoniums in large pots can be an impressive garden feature, a collection of different varieties in

Two large containers of scented pelargoniums make this a popular resting spot at the Royal Horticultural Society garden at Wisley, Surrey, England. Photograph by Andy Van Hevelingen.

small pots, neatly displayed on a bench or plant stand, can be equally captivating. A few plants trained into standards or espaliers can add a vertical element. Such a collection fairly invites you to stop and browse, and the small containers are easy to move indoors for the winter or whenever severe weather threatens.

If the sheer loveliness and landscape value of these fragrant herbs still doesn't provide enough reason for you to put them in your garden, consider their usefulness. Their fragrances can be captured in potpourris, cosmetics, and cuisines. Their foliage, and even the flowers of some cultivars, are a great addition to fresh cut bouquets. And don't overlook their entertainment value: children of all ages can spend many a happy moment stroking the fuzzy, minty leaves of a 'Peppermint' pelargonium.

Growing
Scented
Pelargoniums

POTTING SOIL

SOILS SERVE THE SAME function whether they are in a pot or in your garden—they anchor plants in place and provide nutrients, water, and air to their roots. It is unwise to use garden soil for potted pelargoniums, however. In addition to introducing the risk of soil-borne diseases, garden soil tends to pack down and drain too slowly, depriving the roots of oxygen. Instead, choose a soilless mix, which is sterile and readily available at garden stores. Such mixes typically contain peat moss, perlite, vermiculite, shredded bark and/or washed sand. They are designed to drain rapidly but also hold moisture evenly. If you find that your potting soil stays too wet too long, adding some perlite (a volcanic glass that has been expanded by heat) will improve the drainage. Many growers use a mix of equal parts peat and perlite, sometimes called peatlite. Avoid mixes which contain "topsoil", even if they've been sterilized. We find that they rapidly dry out to the consistency of concrete.

Scented pelargoniums grow best in slightly acid soil, one with a pH between 6.0 and 6.5. Those grown in soils below this range (too acid) may show signs of nutrient toxicity, while those grown in soils above this range (too alkaline) often exhibit signs of nutrient deficiency. Because the soil pH can change over time and may be affected by the addition of fertilizer, we periodically test our potting soil with a pH meter. Unfortunately, good meters cost upwards of $80, and more inexpensive models tend to be unreliable. If you don't have access to a pH meter, but think your soil has "aged" as evidenced by poor plant growth, just repot the plants in fresh potting soil.

POTS AND POTTING

Pots of scented pelargoniums lead
visitors up the steps and into the
Chicago Botanic Garden.
Photograph by Jim Becker.

CONTAINERS OF BOTH CLAY and plastic, the most
common materials used in flowerpots, have advantages and dis-
advantages. While clay pots look great, their porosity may allow
the soil in them to dry out too quickly in hot weather. Plastic pots
are cheaper, lighter in weight, and easier to clean, but they are more
likely to tip over and may keep the soil from drying out as fast as it
should. Some large pots are made of wood or concrete. They may
be attractive but tend to be very heavy and difficult to clean. It
goes without saying that no matter what the pot is made of, it
must have good drainage holes.

Before reusing old pots, remove any old soil and roots. If
you think that they may be contaminated with pests or disease,
discard the soil and roots in a sealed trash bag. Soak the pots for
thirty minutes in a solution of one part chlorine bleach to nine
parts water. Wearing rubber gloves, scrub the pots with a stiff
brush before removing them from the solution. To neutralize the
bleach, rinse the pots in a solution of one part vinegar to nine
parts water and then thoroughly rinse again in plain water.
Sterilizing products made especially for pots and greenhouse
benches and tools can be found in horticultural supply catalogs
(see Sources, page 93).

Start cuttings and seedlings with three or four true leaves in
2- to 3-inch (5- to 8-cm) pots, one to a pot (see Propagation,
page 52). After the plants have filled the pots with roots, usually
in about six weeks, move them into 4-inch (10-cm) pots and allow
them to grow for a few more weeks before transplanting them
into pots that are large enough to hold their mature growth. Most
varieties need a pot that is at least 8 inches (20 cm) wide and 8
inches (20 cm) deep.

This large terra-cotta pot holds a
rosebush underplanted with scented
pelargoniums, heliotrope, and
pineapple mint.
Photograph by Jim Becker.

- *The soil should be just moist.*

- *Never pull a plant out of its pot by tugging on its stem. Instead, spread one hand over the top of the pot holding the stem between your fingers. Then, with the other hand holding the bottom of the pot, turn it upside down. The lower hand should be securely holding both the stem and as much of the soil as possible. Next, sharply but gently bring down a corner of the pot rim onto a firm surface such as a wooden sawhorse or railing. One or two knocks should loosen the root ball enough so that it will slip right out. For pots that are too large to pick up, dig around the root ball with a small, flat trowel or machete, and lift the plant out.*

- *Unless you are removing roots, disturb them as little as possible. Place the plant deep enough in its new pot that you can slightly cover the old soil with new soil. The soil level should be at least 1/2 inch (1 cm) below the rim of the pot so that the water won't spill over the rim when you water.*

Gently break off about one quarter of the old root ball.

Move the plant every year or two into a pot that is just 1" to 2" wider and deeper than the one you are removing it from.

Repot the plant, using new potting soil both under and around the roots.

Plants should be repotted every year or two to give them room to grow new roots and also to refresh the potting mix. Container-grown plants do best when their roots are able to fill the volume of the soil. Unless you are putting several plants into a very large pot or half barrel, move each plant up into a pot that is just 1" to 2" wider and deeper than the one you are removing it from. If you won't be moving the plant to a larger pot, gently break off about one quarter of the old root ball with your fingers or a small tool such as a screwdriver. Repot the plant, using new potting soil both under and around the old roots. You can compost old soil for your garden, but never reuse it for potted plants. Old soil contains too many dead roots, is generally matted and poor in texture, and is unsterile.

WATERING POTTED PLANTS

THE TIMETABLE FOR PROPER watering of scented pelargoniums varies with the season, the weather, the type of pot, the age and variety of the plant, and the location in which it is growing. Mature specimens, especially those that are rootbound, need to be watered much more frequently than do young plants in new soil. Although it may be convenient to water all of your plants at the same time, resist the temptation. They are individuals, and have different water requirements.

As a general rule, water when the top of the soil feels dry. Water each pot thoroughly until you see the excess running out of the drainage holes. This serves both to wet the soil completely and to flush out accumulated salts left from fertilizers. Empty any water that collects in saucers placed under the pots.

Use a hose nozzle or watering can that delivers the water with the least disturbance to the soil. Choose a gentle nozzle for new cuttings and seedlings. Keep water off the foliage and flowers to prevent the spread of disease. Water early in the morning, preferably on a sunny day, so that any wet leaves can dry before nightfall. If you have to stretch to reach your plants, placing the hose nozzle on the end of a metal extension or wand will help direct the water down into the pot and not onto the plant.

Overwatering scenteds promotes soil-borne diseases and weak, soft growth, whereas underwatered

Potted Orange, Concolor Lace, and Rose scenteds for sale at a nursery.
Photograph by Andy Van Hevelingen.

plants are typically short and slow growing and may have yellow, wilted leaves. Although it is better to err on the side of underwatering, it's better still to learn to water properly.

Oddly, pelargoniums cease most growth when the temperature is over 90°F (32°C), and they use less water than at more moderate temperatures. You can sometimes be fooled into overwatering when the top of the soil is dry from evaporation but the root ball is still quite wet. During very hot weather, it is a good idea to pick pots up and feel if the soil is wet (heavy) or dry (light). For very large pots, poke your finger down below the surface to test the moisture level.

Fertilizing Potted Plants

CHANCES ARE, IF YOUR plants aren't growing, you're not fertilizing them properly. Sixteen chemical elements are necessary for healthy plant growth. Three of these, carbon, oxygen, and hydrogen, come from air and water while the rest are supplied by the soil. Of the remaining thirteen, three—nitrogen (N), phosphorus (P), and potassium (K)—are used in relatively large amounts, and are the primary active ingredients in commercial fertilizers. Package labels list the percentage of each, by weight, contained in the mixture. For example, a 15-30-15 fertilizer contains 15 percent nitrogen, 30 percent phosphorus, and 15 percent potassium. You may fertilize scented pelargoniums with a fertilizer that is equally balanced between these elements such as 15-15-15, or one that is a bit higher in phosphorus such as 15-30-15.

Use either water-soluble fertilizers or controlled-release fertilizers which are put on the soil surface as granules. Regular dry fertilizers can burn potted plants and should not be used.

You can control the amount of water-soluble fertilizer your plant gets by varying the frequency of usage and the rate of dilution. Controlled-release fertilizers are designed to yield nutrients slowly over a six month period. They are usually not recommended for use in pots smaller than 6 inches wide. Use both kinds, in tandem, for larger plants and water-solubles only for smaller ones.

During the growing season, which for much of the country is roughly from February to October, apply water-soluble fertilizer at half the manufacturer's recommended dosage every other watering. During the rest of the year, or during extended periods of cool, cloudy weather, use the same fertilizer and dosage once every eight waterings. If you have only a few plants, you can mix the fertilizer in a watering can. If you have many plants to fertilize, use a hose siphon, a device that sucks a concentrated fertilizer solution up from a bucket and then mixes it with water and dispenses it through a regular garden hose. Using a siphon is a real time and back saver.

Controlled-release fertilizers, applied in early spring, should last through the summer. Again, use only about half of the manufacturer's recommended dosage which is determined by the pot size. These fertilizers will provide a steady diet of nutrients, which is useful for those inevitable days when you don't have time to mix and use water-solubles. When sprinkling the fertilizer on the soil, keep it away from the stem. Don't use controlled-release fertilizers during the fall and winter months.

Pelargoniums are heavy feeders of magnesium. A teaspoon (5 ml) of epsom salts (magnesium sulfate) added to each gallon (4 liters) of fertilizer solution every fourth time that you fertilize will provide the necessary extra magnesium.

Although the use of organic fertilizers in garden soils provides great results, they don't work well for container-grown pelargoniums. Manufactured from animal waste products such as fish, bone-, and blood meals, these seem to promote soil-borne diseases and insect pests in pots.

Too little fertilizer can result in yellow leaves and stunted plants. Too much fertilizer may cause growth that is long and spindly. However, these symptoms can also have other causes, such as insufficient light, improper watering, or disease. If you use a balanced fertilizer as recommended above, your plants will get the nutrition they need for healthy growth.

LIGHT AND TEMPERATURE

SUNLIGHT PROVIDES PLANTS WITH the energy they need for photosynthesis and growth. It can be measured both by the number of hours of daylight and by its intensity, factors which are not always under our control. Day length varies throughout the year, with nearly 60 percent less daylight in midwinter than at its peak in midsummer. Clouds and fog can significantly lower the amount of sunlight received even on the longest days.

Because sunlight is also a source of heat, it will raise the temperature of everything that it shines upon. There is nothing more delicious than sitting on a sunporch on a cold winter day, surrounded by scented pelargoniums, and basking in the sun's warmth. But pelargoniums can get too much of a good thing. During the summer, when air temperatures are high, intense sunlight can raise leaf temperatures to dangerous levels, causing them to yellow, curl, or scorch around the edges. Direct sunlight can also heat up the soil in pots to the point at which roots are also damaged.

Your goal is to provide the plants with the maximum amount of light without harming them. The amount of shade that they need depends on your local climate. Parts of coastal California, Oregon, and Washington have such cool, foggy summers that no shade is necessary, whereas growing scented pelargoniums elsewhere in the United States requires the use of shade protection much of the year. Don't shade your pelargoniums by more than 50 percent, about what you'd find in the dappled sunlight under a tree; too much shade promotes weak, soft, and spindly growth. Watch your plants carefully and let them tell you whether they need more sun or shade.

You can shade your greenhouse, patio, or other growing area with fabric, lattice, or climbing plants. Shade fabrics are practical, long lasting, and available at garden stores and from horticultural supply companies. They are woven in different densities, offering from 20% to 90% shade. This allows you to choose the optimum light intensity for your area. If you're not certain which shade density to buy, ask local nursery owners for recommendations.

Pelargoniums grow best at temperatures of 50° to 60°F (10° to 16°C) during the night, and 65° to 75°F (18° to 24°C) during the day. These temperatures approximate those of coastal, Southern California. Those of us living elsewhere have to manipulate our environment as best we can, increasing the amount of shade and ventilation to lower temperatures, decreasing shade and using heaters to raise them.

A planting of mixed scented pelargoniums line a walkway in the Chicago Botanic Garden. Photograph by Jim Becker.

TIPS FOR GROWING SCENTED PELARGONIUMS INDOORS

BRING YOUR POTTED PELARGONIUMS inside when the outdoor nighttime temperatures are still above 45°F (7°C). Don't wait until the weather turns very cold or they will be shocked by the move into the warmer house or greenhouse. Carefully inspect them first and remove any hitchhiking slugs, snails, and other pests.

You don't need a heated sunporch or greenhouse to keep your collection, although these are ideal locations. A south-facing windowsill that receives at least four hours of direct sunlight is adequate. In areas with prolonged cloudy weather, you can supplement the natural light with growlights. These are tubes or bulbs that approximate natural sunlight. These lights should be mounted just a few inches away from the plants and be used for several hours each day. Follow the manufacturer's recommendations for best results.

If your scenteds are planted in beds, it is far easier to winter them over by rooting some cuttings in the early autumn (see Propagation, page 52) than to dig up large plants, pot them, and bring them inside.

Don't crowd potted plants together. They need as much air circulation and sunlight as possible to ensure disease-free healthy growth. Two important winter tasks, inspection for pests and diseases and prompt removal of dead leaves, are much easier to perform when there is some space between the plants.

Scented pelargoniums can go back outdoors in the spring when nighttime temperatures are above 45°F (7°C), and daytime tempera-

A south-facing windowsill that receives at least four hours of direct sunlight is a splendid place to keep your collection during the winter. Photograph by Joe Coca.

tures are again between 60° and 70°F (16° and 21°C). First, harden them off by gradually acclimating them, beginning with several hours a day, to longer periods of exposure. This is a good time to repot and prune older plants and move younger ones up to larger pots.

Tips FOR Growing Scented Pelargoniums IN THE Ground

SCENTED PELARGONIUMS CAN BE grown directly in the ground as a welcome alternative or complement to more common bedding plants. In frost-free areas, they can stay outside year round. They require the same basic care as those grown in pots.

The soil should be fast-draining yet hold moisture; a good garden soil with ample organic matter is ideal. Keep any organic mulches away from the stems, though, to prevent stem rot.

Compost and a well-balanced organic fertilizer, worked well into the soil a few days before planting, are fine for outdoor pelargoniums. Supplement the soil occasionally with liquid fertilizer throughout the growing season. Avoid using raw manures, which are excessively high in nitrogen and promote weak growth, burned roots, and stem rot.

Plant scented pelargoniums in the brightest possible light that will not burn the foliage. In areas with moderate summer temperatures, this can be full sunlight. In hot summer climates, plants will need partial shade in the afternoon. Space the plants so that there is good air circulation between them and room for future growth. This is especially important in areas where summers are humid.

Water the plants when the top inch (2 cm) of soil is dry. Unless you use a drip irrigation system or are very careful with your hose, the foliage will be soaked with each watering. Irrigate early in the morning, preferably on a sunny day, so that the foliage can dry before evening.

Pests are not usually a problem for outdoor plants. However, you should inspect them for pests periodically and take care of any prob-

Mabel Grey and Bitter Lemon. Pelargoniums planted in the ground require the same basic care as those grown in pots. Photograph by Jim Becker.

lems before they get out of hand.

Trim and maintain the plants the same as you would for those grown in pots. (See Pruning, page 36.) If you plan to overwinter them outdoors, don't prune them in the fall to lessen the possibility of cold damage to the base of the stems.

It is difficult to protect outdoor scented pelargoniums during prolonged periods of freezing weather. If you expect only an occasional frosty night, you can cover them in the evening with dry mulch and a sheet of burlap or plastic. You must remove the mulch and covering during the day, however, or the plants will be smothered and will rot.

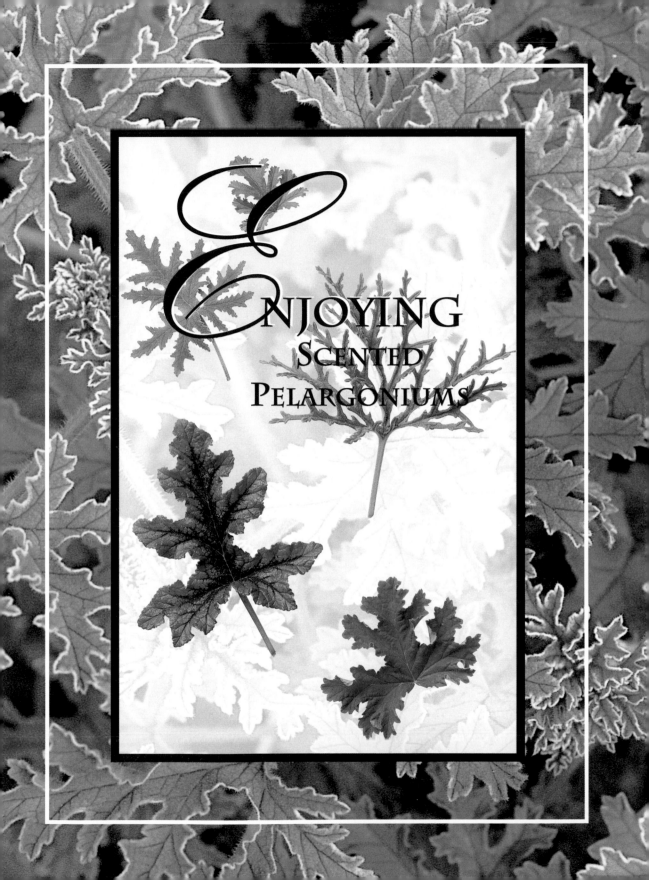

Enjoying Scented Pelargoniums

Pruning

SCENTED PELARGONIUMS THAT ARE not pruned tend to grow long, single stems. These eventually branch out, but the plants then look leggy and often flop over. A few varieties are naturally compact, but for most, careful trimming is necessary to produce plants with full shapes.

Each node has a bud which remains dormant until the tip of the stem it is on is cut off. This is the basis of shaping pelargoniums: remove the tip of one growing stem and several (usually two or three) new stems will begin to grow below the cut.

Begin shaping a pelargonium when it is a newly rooted cutting. As soon as it has at least five nodes or is 4 to 6 inches (10 to 15 cm) tall, cut off its tip, just above the top node with sharp shears or a single-edged razor blade. After the resulting new shoots have also grown four or five nodes long, cut off their tips as well. Repeat this sequence for one more set of newly emerged shoots. Two or three weeks after these final cuts, the plant should have eight to ten growing shoots on a sturdy and attractive framework of branches. The entire series of cuts takes eight to twelve weeks.

Flower buds are produced at the tips of the stems. As soon as you have established the plant's shape, stop trimming and allow it to bloom. This will take another six to eight weeks. Thereafter, maintain the plant by removing old flower stalks and dead leaves. Continue to trim off shoot tips if you wish to encourage further branching.

To keep air circulating throughout the plant, cut off any large mature leaves crowded onto the interior branches. Removing any leaves that touch the soil will help prevent foliar diseases.

Let some branches grow four or five nodes past the point at which you usually trim and shape the plant. Cut them off and root the cuttings to increase your stock.

If you have maintained the shape of your plants throughout the spring and summer, fall pruning isn't necessary. Furthermore, excessive pruning late in the year can be risky because the newly cut stems are susceptible to botrytis, a fungal disease that is common in winter greenhouses.

The best time to prune plants that are a year or more old is late winter or early spring, once they have begun to grow after their winter rest period. Cutting back stems by as much as half their length will stimulate new growth low on the plant and prevent a woody, treelike appearance. As the new growth elongates, cut off some shoot tips to promote branching. This is also the time to move older plants in to larger pots or to repot them.

When the plant has at least five nodes or is 4 to 6 inches (10 to 15 cm) tall, cut off its tip.

When the resulting shoots have four or five nodes, cut off their tips as well.

Two or three weeks after these final cuts, the plant should have eight to ten growing shoots on a sturdy and attractive framework of branches.

CREATING A STANDARD

There are several scented pelargoniums that can be trained into standards. These include *P. citronellum* ('Mabel Grey'), *P. crispum* 'Major', 'Lime', 'Ginger', 'Purple Unique', 'Clorinda', 'Frensham', and 'Lemon Balm'. The techniques are not difficult, but they require patience because the training may take two or three years to complete.

1. Select a young plant that has a straight stem and has never been trimmed.

2. Plant it in a 6-inch (15-cm) clay pot. The weight of clay will help keep the standard from tipping over. This is often a problem in windy areas.

3. As soon as the plant has become well rooted, insert a 24-inch (60-cm) plastic stake or green metal rod into the soil 1/2 inch (1 cm) away from the stem.

4. Cut off all side branches, leaving the tip as the only actively growing shoot. Also cut off any leaves that rub against the stake. Make all cuts with thin, sharp shears and don't leave a stub.

5. Tie the stem up against the stake with raffia, cotton string, plant tie ribbon, or narrow strips of pantyhose. Make ties every inch (2 cm), adding new ones as the plant grows. The ties must be secure but not so tight as to damage the stem. You may have to retie them as the stem increases in girth.

6. When the tip has grown to the top of the stake, cut off the top node, which will stimulate the plant to branch out. Let the new shoots that emerge from the top four nodes develop, but remove all the others below them.

7. After the new shoots have grown three or four nodes long, trim off their tips. Continue to grow and trim new shoots in this manner until they have formed a round framework of branches. A rule of proportion for standards is that the diameter of the ball of foliage should be about one-third to one-half the height of the plant. In this example, it should be 6 to 9 inches (15 to 23 cm) wide.

8. Maintain the shape by carefully trimming the new growth and by removing all lower shoots and leaves.

9. Care for the standard as you do your other potted pelargoniums. As soon as the stem is strong enough to support itself, you may remove the stake by cutting it off at ground level.

CREATING AN ESPALIER

Pelargonium espaliers are not as commonly seen as standards, but they can make a spectacular display, especially when the plant has showy flowers such as those of 'Clorinda' or interesting foliage such as that of 'Peppermint'. The best choices for espaliers are pelargoniums with sprawling growth. Espaliers need not be as precisely shaped as standards, and they tolerate mistakes and accidents more gracefully. You can start with young plants, but the easiest way to create an espalier is to start with a plant that already has long stems.

The annual show of the Los Angeles Pelargonium and Geranium Society, held each Mother's Day, usually displays some exquisitely trained espaliers as well as specimens of numerous cultivars. If you are in the area, don't miss it.

1. Select a mature plant with stems a foot (30 cm) or more long, and that has been growing in a pot at least 6 inches (15 cm) wide.

2. Pot up the plant into a large wooden or clay container. Insert a trellis, 3 to 4 feet (1 m) high. Use a trellis made of rot-resistant or treated wood, plastic, or metal.

3. Gently lean the plant onto the trellis, and spread out its branches. Loosely tie them onto the structure with raffia or stretchable plastic ties. Do not use wire ties which will cut into the stems as they increase in girth.

4. Train the branches to follow the shape of the trellis. Trim off the stem ends if more branching is needed to fill out the frame. When the branches approach the top of the trellis, cut off their tips to control their height and encourage fuller growth.

5. Maintain the espalier by removing stray branches and carefully trimming new growth.

Pelargoniums IN THE Home

WITH SUCH A WONDERFULLY scented group of plants, it is not surprising that there are so many different ways to keep their fragrances and flavors alive throughout the year. Here are some ideas to get you started.

IN THE KITCHEN

Not all scented pelargoniums have tastes that complement cookery. Recipes call for either rose, lemon, or mint. Most often their flavors are infused into the dish and they are removed and discarded before serving, although fresh leaves can be used as a decorative garnish.

The leaves are used fresh, another good reason to keep a few plants indoors during the winter. Avoid using pesticides on plants destined for kitchen use. If your plants have insects, wash them off the leaves before harvest.

Scenteds are typically used in sweet dishes. Rose varieties add a delicate but stimulating flavor to sugar which is then used in baked goods or to sweeten teas. Stack clean, dry leaves in a large canister between 1-inch (2-cm) layers of sugar. Place the canister in a warm spot for two to four weeks, and then sift out the leaves. Some cooks recommend first bruising the leaves to impart more flavor, but Rosetta Clarkson, in her classic book *Magic Gardens* (New York: Macmillan, 1992) had a more ingenious idea. She carefully dried her rose- and peppermint-scented pelargonium leaves together with rosebuds between the sugar layers the way other people often do with sand. Not only did they flavor the sugar, but the perfectly dried leaves and buds could be brushed off and used in potpourri jars or other decorations.

Rose-flavored pelargonium sugar can be substituted for all or part of the plain sugar called for in recipes for white cakes or icings. Small rose- or lemon-scented leaves can also be candied by dipping them in egg white and coating them with sugar to create impressive cake decorations. Dry them on a rack before using.

Scented pelargoniums can add flavor to cakes in other ways, too. Arrange them in the bottom of a lined or buttered baking pan and pour the batter over them. Jellies flavored with rose-scenteds can be used as a filling for sponge- or angel-cake layers. Apple and crab-apple jellies are most commonly used for this purpose. Dunk tied bunches of leaves repeatedly into the jelly just before removing it from the heat, or pour hot jelly into jars in which you have placed a few leaves. These jellies are also tasty on toast and hot biscuits.

Scented Pelargoniums make a cup of tea more memorable. Photograph by Joe Coca.

Other culinary uses for scenteds include fruit punches, wine cups, ice cream, and sorbets. Herbal vinegars add zest to salads, vinaigrettes, marinades, and almost anything else that calls for vinegar. Use lemon- and rose-scented pelargoniums in sweet vinegar recipes; they combine especially well with lemon verbena, lemon basil, and mints.

Scented pelargoniums can make a cup of tea more memorable. Try steeping a couple of rose-, lemon-, or peppermint-scented leaves in a pot of black tea. Add a few cloves if you like along with orange or lemon slices and serve the tea either hot or iced. Leaves of lemon-scented pelargoniums may be added to other citrus-flavored herbs, such as lemon verbena, lemon balm, or orange mint, for a strictly herbal tea blend. Try freezing small leaves of lemon- or mint-scenteds in ice-cube trays to add flavor and beauty to iced teas and punches.

The recipe for this luscious cake is the work of Adelma Simmons of Caprilands Herb Farm, Coventry, Connecticut.

ROSE PELARGONIUM CREAM CAKE

1 cup (240 ml) whipping cream
1 cup (240 ml) sugar
2 eggs
1 1/2 cups (360 ml) flour

2 teaspoons (10 ml) baking powder
1 teaspoon (5 ml) vanilla extract
Rose pelargonium leaves, freshly picked

Whip the whipping cream until stiff. Add the of sugar slowly and beat until blended. Add the eggs, one at a time, beating after each addition. Sift the flour, add the baking powder, sift again, and fold into the egg and cream mixture. Whip in the vanilla extract. Butter two 8-inch (20 cm) layer cake tins and line the bottoms and sides with rose pelargonium leaves. Pour the batter over the leaves, which will be held in place by the butter in the tin. Bake at 375°F (190°C) until golden brown on top. Frost with Rose Pelargonium Frosting.

ROSE PELARGONIUM FROSTING

4 rose pelargonium leaves
2 cups (475 ml) confectioner's sugar
1 egg white

1 teaspoon (5 ml) lemon juice
1 drop vanilla extract
Small pelargonium leaves for garnish

Macerate four leaves in a mortar and pestle until all fibers are broken. Add to the confectioner's sugar. Beat the egg white with a whisk until frothy. Add it, lemon juice and vanilla extract to the sugar. Whip until smooth and spread on the cooled cake. Decorate with small pelargonium leaves pressed into the frosting.

From *Tea and Tranquillity,* by Adelma Simmons (Tolland, Connecticut: Clinton Press, 1990).

This Rose pelargonium cream cake has fresh leaves lining the bottoms of the layers, incorporated in the frosting, and used as garnish. Photograph by Joe Coca.

Sweet Rice with Rose Pelargonium

Serves 6

1 cup (240 ml) round-grain rice
2 cups (475 ml) milk
8 rose pelargonium leaves
1 ounce (30 g) dry coconut

2 ounces (60 g) flaked almonds
2 ounces (60 g) raisins
1 cup (240 ml) soft brown sugar

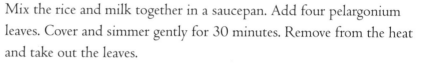

Mix the rice and milk together in a saucepan. Add four pelargonium leaves. Cover and simmer gently for 30 minutes. Remove from the heat and take out the leaves.

Preheat the oven to 375°F (190°C). Add the coconut, almonds, raisins, and sugar to the milk mixture, stirring well. Transfer the mixture to an 8-inch (20-cm) ovenproof dish. Arrange the remaining pelargonium leaves across the top. Bake for 45 minutes.

From *The Complete Book of Herbs,* by Leslie Bremness (New York: Viking Studio Books, 1988)

Sorbet of Rose Pelargonium and Sweet Cicely

This exquisite sorbet was developed by Ron Zimmerman of the Herbfarm in Fall City, Washington. It is best made in midsummer, when rose pelargonium leaves are richest in essential oils. Leaves of sweet cicely (Myrrhis odorata) lend just a hint of anise and reduce the amount of sugar needed.

3 1/2 cups (830 ml) water
1 5/8 (390 ml) cups sugar
24 rose pelargonium leaves

24 six-inch (15-cm) sprigs sweet cicely
1/2 cup (120 ml) lemon juice

In a saucepan, combine the water with 1 1/4 cups (300 ml) of the sugar and bring to a boil. Boil 5 minutes, then cool to room temperature. Place the rose pelargonium leaves, sweet cicely sprigs, and remaining 3/8 cup (90 ml) of sugar in a food processor fitted with a steel blade. Process 3 minutes. Combine the herbal puree with the cooled syrup, stir, and let stand 1 hour.

Strain the mixture through a fine sieve or several layers of cheesecloth. Add the lemon juice. Freeze in an ice cream maker according to the manufacturer's directions. Alternatively, pour the mixture into a metal bowl and place it in the freezer. Scrape down the sides every hour or so until the sorbet is fully frozen, in 3 to 4 hours. Serve in chilled glasses garnished with a rose pelargonium blossom.

Scented pelargonium sorbet prepared in the freezer makes a refreshing treat reminiscent of Italian ice.
Photograph by Joe Coca.

POTPOURRI

The dried leaves of scented pelargoniums are an excellent addition to potpourri. The fragrances most commonly used are rose, lemon/citrus, and mint. Dry the leaves on racks in a spot out of direct sunlight that has good air circulation and a temperature between 70° and 90°F (21° and 32°). They are ready when the petioles (leaf stems) break with a snap.

The leaves tend to curl as they dry. You can preserve the delicate shape of the finely cut kinds such as 'Old-Fashioned Rose' by drying them in sand, silica gel, or even sugar (see page 42), or by pressing them in a flower press. These preserved leaves make lovely decorative touches inside glass potpourri jars and in pressed floral pictures. Although their color will fade, their sharp silhouette more than makes up for the color loss.

Add the leaves to any of your favorite potpourri recipes. Substitute the lemon-scenteds for lemon herbs, the rose-scenteds for true rose petals, or create your own mixes. This recipe, created at Hinode Farm, makes a delightfully refreshing potpourri.

*2 cups (475 ml) rose-scented
  pelargonium leaves*
*1 cup (240 ml) lavender flowers,
  preferably left on the stem*
1 cup (240 ml) lemon-scented herbs

2 cups (475 ml) rose petals
1 cup (240 ml) oakmoss
1 cup (240 ml) larkspur petals
1 cup (240 ml) rosemary leaves
A few small spruce or fir cones

For a sharper fragrance, mix 50 drops rose pelargonium oil with 6 tablespoons (40 ml) orrisroot (cut and sifted), and add this mixture to the potpourri. Orrisroot is a fixative, a substance that helps make the fragrance last longer.

Sachets are bags or pillows made from finely woven cloth and stuffed with ground potpourri. They provide an easy way to keep the fragrance of herbs wafting about the house from drawers, closets, seat cushions, or tables. Mrs. C. W. Earle, in *Potpourri From a Surrey Garden*, noted, "On the backs of my armchairs are thin Liberty silk oblong bags, like miniature saddle bags, filled with dried lavender, sweet verbena, and sweet geranium leaves. The visitor who leans back in his chair wonders from where the sweet scent comes.

Old Fashioned-Rose, interplanted with lavender being harvested at Hinode Farm, Gold Hill, Oregon, for use in potpourri. Photograph by Jim Becker.

Potpourri prepared with flowers, scented pelargonium leaves, and other herbs. Photograph by Joe Coca.

Floral Designs

The flowers of scented pelargoniums last but a couple of days in fresh bouquets, but the long stems of foliage keep for weeks and add interesting shapes, colors, textures, and fragrances to floral designs.

The foliage has been a favorite ingredient of tussie-mussies, the traditional, small bouquets made from fresh herbs and flowers. The stems are bound up just below the flowers and foliage, giving these bouquets a somewhat flat-topped appearance.

Because they are both handmade and sentimental, tussie-mussies make wonderful little gifts. They are often presented with the stems placed through an opening cut into a paper doily and with festive ribbons tied about the base.

Tussie-mussie created by Geraldine Adamich Laufer, author of *Tussie-Mussies* **(New York: Workman Publishing, 1993).**
Photograph by Chipp Jamison.

Beyond
the Basics

PROPAGATION

THE TERM "PROPAGATION" INCLUDES all of the ways of increasing the numbers of plants. The two most common ways to propagate scented pelargoniums are by seeds and stem cuttings.

SEED PROPAGATION

The true species can be grown from seeds, which is of course their natural means of reproduction. For some, such as 'Apple' (*P. odoratissimum*), 'Coconut' (*P. grossularioides*), and 'Upright Coconut' (*P. elongatum*), seeds are also the easiest method of propagation, as their stems are quite short and not very suitable for cuttings.

In their natural habitat, a large population of a species will show a range of variation. For instance, in South Africa, 'Coconut' plants may have pink, white, or magenta flowers. Some plants of 'Apple' may have a typical fruity scent whereas others smell minty. In your garden, however, you can expect the species to come true from seed unless they have been cross-pollinated by other species or cultivars. Fortunately, chance cross-pollination seldom produces viable seeds although it can occur where different species are closely intermingled, as in greenhouses.

If your seedlings should grow into plants that look different from their parent species, don't label them with the parental name. Such seed-produced variations are the origin of many new cultivars. We'll discuss this topic further in the chapter on hybridization (page 59).

Seeds of scented pelargoniums are seldom listed in mail-order catalogs, but you can collect them from your own plants. Each of the five carpels in a floret contains a single seed. When the seeds are ripe, the carpels begin slowly to detach from each other, starting at the seed end. The seeds are ready to harvest when the carpels turn brown and a dark line runs up the style. As the carpels continue to separate, they stretch outward and remain attached only at the tips of their now-feathery styles. This is your last chance to collect the seeds before they blow away.

Place the harvested carpels in a paper bag and let them dry for several days. You can plant the entire carpel or first remove the seed by gently rubbing the carpels between your hands. Pick away the resulting chaff or put the seeds through a sieve. Store any seeds which you don't plant immediately in air-tight glass jars in a cool, dark location. The seeds will remain viable for one to three years, depending on the species.

Follow these instructions for starting scented pelargoniums from seeds.

1. Select a container that is rigid, is at least 6 inches (15 cm) wide and 2 inches (5 cm) deep, and has good drainage holes. Avoid using containers made of pressed fibers as they dry out too quickly.

2. Fill the container with a soilless mix (see page 20). Lightly settle the soil with your fingers and water the container until the excess trickles out the drainage holes. The soil level should come to at least 1/2 inch (1 cm) below the rim.

3. With a pencil, make holes for the seeds that are 1 to 2 inches (2 to 5 cm) apart and at a depth equal to twice the diameter of the seed.

4. Place a seed in each hole and lightly cover it with additional soilless mix.

5. With a misting nozzle, water the container carefully so as not to wash the seeds out of their holes or bury them too deeply.

6. Place the planted container in a sunny location or under grow lights. To keep the soil evenly moist, cover the container loosely with a piece of glass. Lift the glass each day to allow excess moisture to escape and remove it completely after the first seedlings appear.

7. For best germination, the soil temperature should be between 70° and 80°F (21° and 27°C). Use a heating mat if necessary.

8. Seedlings should emerge in two to three weeks. After they have grown a pair of true leaves, begin to fertilize with a mild, water soluble fertilizer. (See Fertilizing Potted Plants, page 26.)

9. When the seedlings have three or four leaves, cut the soil between them with a sharp knife or gently tease them apart. Transplant each seedling into a 2- to 3-inch (5- to 8-cm) pot, holding it by a leaf, not by the stem. Set it slightly deeper than it was in the germinating container so that the roots are completely covered with soil. Gently press the soil around the stem before watering.

10. Place the newly transplanted seedlings in partial shade for a few days, and then gradually, over a ten-day period, acclimatize them to full light.

PROPAGATION FROM STEM CUTTINGS

To ensure that the offspring are identical to their parents, cultivars must be propagated by stem cuttings. While this method is not complicated, it is not foolproof either. The following tips will help you to achieve success.

1. Fill a 2½-inch (6-cm) pot with a soilless mix (see page 20) for each cutting that you plan to take. Very lightly settle the mix with your fingers and then water the pot until the excess trickles out of the drainage holes. The soil should now be about 1/2 inch (1 cm) below the rim of the pot.

2. Select a healthy, established stock plant from which to take the cuttings.

3. Select actively growing shoots that are firm and not floppy. You can take cuttings throughout the growing season, but success is more certain in spring and fall. Don't use the older, woody (brown) portions of the stem. Each cutting should

include at least three stem nodes, but four or five are better. A node is the point on the stem at which the leaves are attached.

4. With a single-edged razor blade (especially good for thick stems) or very sharp, scissor-type gardening shears, make your cut just above a node on the stock plant. If the stems are long enough and you need more propagating material, you can also take cuttings below the tip. Don't leave a stub: it can become a target for disease.

5. Recut the cutting to just below its lowest node. This is the spot where root formation is best.

6. Remove the leaves from the stem that will be under or close to the soil surface. It is best to bury at least two or three nodes. Also remove any stipules that are found at the base of the leaf stems, since these can rot if buried.

7. With a sharpened pencil, make a hole in the center of the soilless mix deep enough to bury the lower nodes and insert the cutting. Settle the soil around the cutting by gently rewatering the pot.

8. Place the potted cuttings in a spot out of the wind or direct sunlight. If the weather is cool, place them on a heating mat. Rooting is quickest and most successful when the soil temperature is 70° to 80°F (21° to 27°C). The soil should be kept evenly moist through out the rooting season.

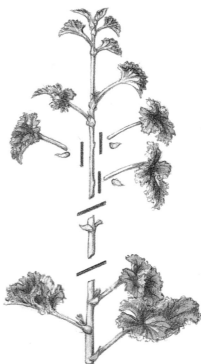

Here are some important don'ts:

1. Don't bother with rooting hormones; the cuttings root just as well without them.

2. Don't let the ends of the cuttings dry out before you stick them into the soil. Despite the recommendations in some older books to leave the cuttings to dry overnight before sticking, this practice yields poor results.

3. Don't snap the cuttings off the stock plant: snapping damages the stock plant and makes it susceptible to diseases. It also produces poor cuttings.

4. Don't root several cuttings in a single pot. You'll just have to tease them apart later, resulting in transplant shock, delayed growth, and time wasted on unnecessary transplanting.

If any leaves turn yellow or become mildewed, remove immediately. Also, cut off any flower buds that form, as they only draw needed energy away from the cuttings.

Rooting should occur within three to four weeks. When it does, you'll see signs of new bud and leaf growth. At this stage, begin to fertilize the cuttings with a mild, water-soluble fertilizer. (See Fertilizing Potted Plants, page 26.) Place the plants in brighter light for one to two weeks before exposing them to full sunlight.

Variegations

VARIEGATED SCENTED PELARGONIUMS ARE those whose foliage is marked with different colors such as cream, white, gold, or chartreuse. In some, such as 'Snowflake', the color is randomly splashed across the leaf in a hit or miss pattern. In others, the color appears only on the leaf margin. This edging may be broad, as in 'Charity', narrow, as in 'Grey Lady Plymouth', or of varying widths, as in 'Lady Plymouth'.

Variegations usually come about when an actively growing shoot on an otherwise normal plant undergoes a genetic mutation. The mutated shoot, called a "sport", continues to grow with the abnormal color pattern while the rest of the plant remains unchanged.

The discovery of such sports can lead to new cultivars. Two recent examples are 'Golden Lemon Crispum', a sport of *P. crispum* found growing at WellSweep Herb Farm in New Jersey, and 'Phyllis', which was discovered in England on a plant of 'Paton's Unique' (also known as 'Apricot'). Both of these show attractive edge variegations, the former being yellow/green and the latter pure white.

Variegated Nutmeg

If one of your plants produces a sport, you may remove it from the stock plant and propagate the cutting. Do realize, though, that if a particular pelargonium sported on your plant, it might also, as often happens, sport in a similar way on someone else's plant. Before you name your "new" cultivar, consult scented pelargonium authorities to find out whether a like variety already exists. You can minimize the confusion caused by grower's giving different names to the same sport by simply adding the word "variegated" to the cultivar from which a sport arose. For instance, a sport of the cultivar 'Attar of Roses' propagated in the Brawner greenhouse will be introduced as 'Variegated Attar of Roses'.

Sports can also develop from other sports. 'Snowflake', with its

Golden Nutmeg

Variegated Prince Rupert

hit-or-miss white variegation, came from the all-green 'Round Leaf Rose'. 'Atomic Snowflake', which has a gold variegation and a slightly distorted leaf edge, is a sport of 'Snowflake'.

Sometimes variegated plants develop shoots which are either all green or all white. This is because the mutation is not entirely stable. The green shoots, called reversions, are identical to the plant from which the sport originated. This is another reason why its useful to know the origin of variegated cultivars. If shoots of 'Variegated Attar of Roses' revert, we know that these all-green forms are simply 'Attar of Roses' and aren't tempted to rename them. Remove reversions from the plant as they are often very vigorous and can soon overpower the variegated form. Discard any all-white "ghost" shoots, too, as they lack chlorophyll and will only die if you attempt to propagate them.

Reversions may also develop from the roots of variegated pelargoniums. These should likewise be cut away and not used for propagation.

When you take cuttings from variegated plants for propagation, choose ones with good color. Avoid those which have just a hint of the variegation showing. Some cultivars, such as 'Peach', frequently lose the color in their shoots and must be carefully propagated so that you can replace these plants with new ones with the proper appearance.

Hybridization

HYBRIDIZATION IS THE PRODUCTION of offspring from parents of different genetic makeup. In plants, it is achieved by cross-pollination: the transfer of pollen from the anther of one plant to the stigma of another. The pollen grains germinate on the stigma and grow down the style into the ovary where fertilization occurs and seeds develop. The plant that donates the pollen is called the pollen parent, and the one that receives the pollen is the seed parent. The offspring of such crosses are called hybrids.

Much of the diversity among scented pelargoniums happens by chance. Pollinating insects, such as bees, are natural, though inadvertent hybridizers. Because they visit hundreds of flowers each day, the parentage of any seeds that result from their efforts is always unknown.

People have learned to duplicate the pollinating skills of insects but with a big difference: they can carefully choose the parent plants, intentionally creating a new plant or improving the characteristics of an existing one. For instance, if you had a scented pelargonium with lovely blooms but an ungainly appearance, you might cross it with one that has nice, compact growth, hoping that the resulting hybrid would have both attractive form and flowers. Of course, successful plant breeding is seldom this simple. Though you might get lucky on the first try, it often takes hundreds of crosses and many years of work to achieve the desired results.

As mentioned earlier, many varieties of scented pelargoniums are so dissimilar genetically that they will not produce viable seeds when cross-pollinated. Discovering which cultivars will readily hybridize is often a matter of trial and error, so just have fun and give it a try.

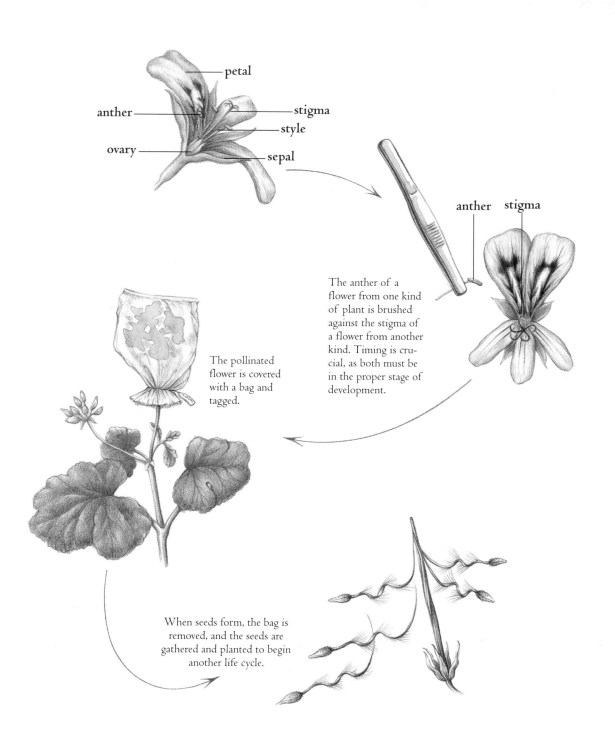

petal

anther

stigma

style

ovary

sepal

anther   stigma

The anther of a
flower from one kind
of plant is brushed
against the stigma of
a flower from another
kind. Timing is cru-
cial, as both must be
in the proper stage of
development.

The pollinated
flower is covered
with a bag and
tagged.

When seeds form, the bag is
removed, and the seeds are
gathered and planted to begin
another life cycle.

Here's how:

1. Carefully select the parent plants. The stigma of a flower is receptive for only a few days or even hours; this time must coincide with the time that another plant is producing pollen. A 10X hand lens is helpful in gauging flower development: ripe pollen looks like flour, and a receptive stigma appears sticky. Avoid any flower that already has pollen grains on its stigma, but don't worry if a flower's pollen falls on its own stigma. In scented pelargoniums, pollen usually develops after the time that the stigma is receptive—nature's way of discouraging self-pollination.

2. With tweezers, grasp a stamen of the pollen parent just below the anther. Carry it over to the seed parent and brush its pollen onto all five arms of the stigma of the seed parent. You may need more than one stamen to supply enough pollen.

3. After pollinating the flower, cover it with a small, fine-mesh bag to keep out pollinating insects and windblown pollen. Small, drawstring muslin tea bags (available at health-food stores) or empty, unused paper tea bags work well. Secure the bottom of the bag with cotton string and tag the flower with an identification number. Careful record keeping is important for evaluating hybrids and in planning future crosses. Clean tweezers with alcohol before reusing them.

4. If fertilization is successful, seeds will soon form. Remove the sack after a week or two, then gather the seeds when they are ripe and plant them (see pages 52–54).

5. Carefully evaluate the resulting seedlings. Grow the plants for a year or more and look objectively at their performance and appearance. If they seem gardenworthy, you can consult pelargonium authorities to see if a similar hybrid is already available.

DISEASES

SCENTED PELARGONIUMS ARE NOT particularly prone to diseases, provided you give them proper care. Most diseases are deterred by good ventilation, careful watering, use of sterile pots and potting soil, and the prompt removal of dead leaves. Above all, buy disease-free stock plants. As not all diseases are easy to detect, your purchasing decisions will have to be based as much on the reputation of the grower as on your inspection of their plants. In some cases, a fungicide is necessary for disease control. Carefully follow the label instructions and wear protective gear—gloves, goggles, and a respirator designed specifically for use with fungicides and pesticides.

Geraniums IV (Batavia, Illinois: Ball Publishing, 1993), a reference book written primarily for the commercial nursery trade, lists twenty-four diseases of pelargoniums. Fortunately, most people will never see more than a few of these. The following are some of the more common ones that affect scented pelargoniums. For absolute identification, always consult your local agricultural extension agent, who will advise you of the proper procedures for taking and delivering infected samples. If you do not have an agent in your area, contact the Horticulture Department of your state university.

BOTRYTIS

The fungal disease *Botrytis cinerea* is called gray mold or stem, leaf, or flower blight, depending upon which part of the plant is infected. It is the most common disease of pelargoniums and is often found in greenhouses during the winter. It spreads by tiny, seedlike spores, which germinate in cool (60° to 75°F (16° to 24°C)), humid conditions. The spores can be spread by air, water, plant-to-plant contact, and tools or hands that have touched infected plants.

Symptoms: The first parts of the plant usually infected are older leaves and flowers. These become soft and covered with a powdery gray mold. As the condition worsens, vigorous leaves and stems may be affected. In the most extreme cases, the disease can kill the entire plant, but this happens only if the problem is ignored.

Control: Avoid wetting the leaves and flowers when watering. Increase the air circulation around plants by spacing them farther apart and by using fans. Remove all dead or fallen leaves and cut off spent flowers before the petals drop off. Remove all infected stems, leaves, and flowers, being careful not to cut directly into the infected areas. Discard diseased material in sealed trash bags.

If these measures do not control the disease, a fungicide should be used.

Verticillium Wilt

This fungal disease, *Verticillium albo-atrum,* spreads through the soil and attacks a plant's circulatory system. Infected plants may not show any symptoms for weeks or even months.

Symptoms: An infected plant will appear to be wilted even though the soil is moist. Leaves may turn yellow and the growth may be stunted, conditions that resemble nutrient deficiencies, underwatering, or pythium root rot (see page 64).

Control: Always use sterile soil, pots, and digging tools. Plants which show abnormal wilting should be immediately isolated. This reduces the risk of infected soil accidentally moving into adjacent pots via splashing, tools, or other means. Do not take cuttings from plants suspected of having the disease. Laboratory testing is necessary for an accurate diagnosis. Discard infected plants and their soil in sealed trash bags.

Geranium Rust

The fungal disease *Puccinia pelargonii-zoralis* is rapidly spread by spores which are carried by wind, splashing water, and hands. The spores can germinate on the leaves only if water is present. Although it is more commonly seen on zonal and regal pelargoniums, it can also infect the

scenteds. In the United States, it is most frequently seen on the Pacific coast.

Symptoms: Small yellow spots appear on the undersides of the leaves, and these soon produce the rust-colored spores. A ring of fungus grows around each original spot, giving it the appearance of a bulls-eye. The disease can also spread to the upper side of the leaves.

Control: Periodically check the undersides of leaves, especially during wet or damp weather. Cut off and discard infected leaves. Also, follow the preventive measures recommended for botrytis. In severe cases, use a fungicide, following the manufacturer's directions.

PYTHIUM ROOT ROT

This is the most common of several fungal diseases that attack and kill roots. It can remain dormant in the soil for as long as twelve years.

Symptoms: The infection starts at the root tips, which die and turn brown. Because the plant cannot take in water and nutrients efficiently, it can appear wilted, with yellowed leaves and stunted growth despite being given proper care.

Control: The disease is very difficult to control once it has begun. Prevention is the best cure. Always use sterilized pots, soil, and digging tools. Discard infected plants along with their soil in sealed trash bags. Sterilize surfaces that may have come in contact with the plant's pot or soil.

BLACK LEG

This is a fungal disease that attacks newly rooted cuttings.

Symptoms: A brown, slimy, shiny area develops at the base of the cutting. This soon turns black and can progress up the stem, killing the cutting.

Control: Use the measures outlined for pythium root rot.

Bacterial Blight

This disease is caused by the bacterium *Xanthomonas campestre pelargonii.* It is highly contagious, destructive, and incurable, causing millions of dollars in loses to commercial nurseries each year. The disease is often spread when cuttings are taken from symptomless stock plants. It also spreads by leaf-to-leaf contact and by water dripping from infected leaves, tools, or hands.

Symptoms: Infected plants may not show any symptoms immediately, but infected leaves may show spots, yellowing, or wilting similar to fungal diseases. Infected stems eventually turn brown or black and rot. A laboratory test is necessary to make an accurate diagnosis.

Control: Isolate all plants suspected of having the disease at once. Sterilize any tools, containers, or surfaces that may have come into contact with diseased plants. Discard all infected plants and their soil in sealed trash bags. Do not take cuttings from infected plants.

PESTS

ONLY A FEW PESTS attack scented pelargoniums, and these are a problem primarily when the plants are grown indoors. Managing pests is not difficult if you maintain proper growing conditions and keep a watchful eye on the plants. Problems spotted before they become infestations are relatively easy to control.

To make effective use of pesticides, you must first identify the pest and know its habits.

Don't be fooled into thinking that if a little pesticide is good, a lot is better. Needless use of pesticides is harmful to you, the plants, and the environment, and it is expensive, too. Many pesticides are relatively safe to use but only if you follow the instructions on the labels and wear protective gear: gloves, goggles, and a respirator designed specifically for use with fungicides and pesticides.

Here are a few common pests and recommendations for their control. For information about a broader range of pests, consult one of the books listed in the Bibliography.

APHIDS

Aphids are small (1/10" to 1/2" (1/4 to 1¼ cm)) long , pear-shaped bugs that suck out plant juices. They may be green, black, yellow, red, or brown, and some have wings. They are usually found under leaves or crowded onto the tips of growing shoots. Ants are often found in the company of aphids, attracted by a sweet liquid that the aphids excrete. Aphids are found both outdoors during the growing season and indoors throughout the year. They reproduce rapidly.

Symptoms: Aphids are easy to spot

with the naked eye. A black sooty mold, which grows on leaves covered with their excretions, is another sign of their presence.

Control: Insecticidal soaps or liquid pyrethrum sprays work well. Apply every few days for about two weeks.

WHITEFLIES

Whiteflies (*Trialeurodes vaporariorum*) resemble tiny white moths. They are only 1/20 inch (1.27 mm) long, and live mainly on the underside of leaves, where they lay their eggs. They are often found in greenhouses and are especially troublesome during warm weather.

Symptoms: The adults flutter about when the plant leaves are disturbed. The flat white larvae (nymphs) and eggs can be seen with a magnifying glass on the underside of the leaves. Whiteflies also excrete a sweet liquid which can cause the growth of a black sooty mold. In extreme infestations, leaves may wither and drop off. The adults are attracted to sticky yellow or blue traps, which are available at garden stores, and these can be used for their early detection.

Control: Insecticidal soaps and liquid pyrethrum sprays are effective against the flying adults. Horticultural oil spray will kill eggs and nymphs and is a good follow-up to use after the adults have been controlled. Concentrate all sprays on the underside of the leaves.

SPIDER MITES

These creatures are minute, 1/100 inch (.025 mm) long, and resemble and are related to spiders. They are best observed with a magnifying glass or 10X hand lens. There are several species of spider mites; some are reddish, while others are tan with dark spots. They are found mainly on the undersides of leaves and are especially prevalent in greenhouses. They do not fly but crawl or are blown from plant to plant.

Symptoms: Heavy infestations destroy the leaves, which appear finely speckled with white or brown. They also produce a fine webbing that is often easy to spot.

Control: Light horticultural oils are effective against both the eggs and the adults, while insecticidal soaps work well only on the adults. Either should be applied about once a week until the pests are gone.

MEALYBUGS

Adult mealybugs are small, oval insects with a spiny, waxy white covering. They feed by sucking out plant juices; some types feed on the roots and others, on the leaves and stems. The foliar types are often visible as cottonlike masses in the leaf axils or on buds. Root mealybugs are occasionally found near the soil surface but more commonly are detected on the root ball when a plant is removed from its pot. A white, telltale residue may be noticed on the inside of the pot.

Symptoms: Shoots or leaves may become wilted and infected plants may be stunted and nutrient deficient. They may eventually die.

Control: Mealybugs' waxy coating provides some protection from pesticides, making them difficult to control. Swab foliar types with rubbing alcohol. Several applications may be necessary. Insecticidal soaps may be used, but they are not entirely effective. The only product currently registered for the control of root mealybugs is Enstar II, which works by disrupting the insect's life cycle with a high dosage of its own growth hormones. Unfortunately, it is expensive and available only through horticultural supply catalogs. The most practical control measure for root mealybugs is to take cuttings from the healthy stems and then dispose of the infested plants and their soil in sealed trash bags.

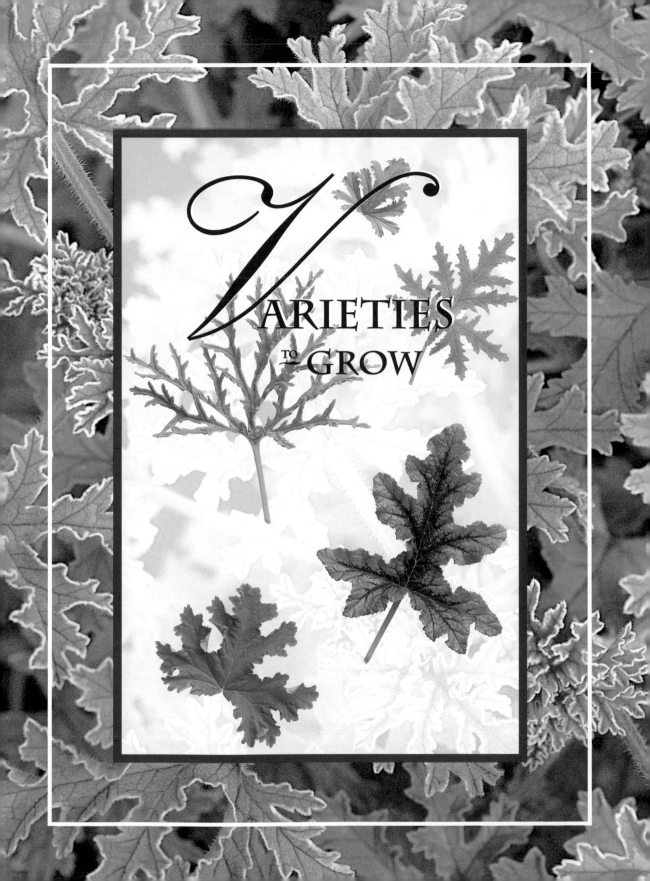

VARIETIES TO GROW

Atomic Snowflake

Attar of Roses

Both's Snowflake

Of the dozens of scented pelargoniums offered by nurseries and listed in plant catalogs, we discuss here only the best: scenteds that we deem to have a nice aroma, a pretty flower, and/or a good growth habit. We feel that these are most likely to bring you peak enjoyment of these fascinating plants.

ROSE-SCENTED

The rose-scenteds are probably the most popular of scented pelargoniums. The group contains a few true species, but most of its members are cultivars. Which one has the "truest" rose fragrance is a matter of debate, but 'Old-Fashioned Rose' or 'Attar of Roses' are the chief contenders. The scent of *P. capitatum* varies from good to nonexistent. Rose-scenteds are grown commercially in Africa, France, and Réunion for their oil, which is used in the perfume and cosmetics industries.

The fragrance of some members of the rose-scented have a citruslike overtone, which is termed lemon-rose. The predominant scent varies with the cultivar.

'ATOMIC SNOWFLAKE'

This sport of 'Snowflake' has a gold variegation, and a slightly distorted leaf edge. The lavender flower and lemon-rose scent are identical to those of 'Snowflake'. It will also revert to 'Round-Leaf Rose' but less readily than will 'Snowflake'.

'ATTAR OF ROSES'

This fairly large plant with three-lobed leaves and a nice, strong rose scent is a good choice for sachets and potpourri. The small flowers are lavender.

'BOTH'S SNOWFLAKE' ('ICE CRYSTAL ROSE')

Leaves are gray-green and deeply divided, with irregular splashes of cream and white. Strong lemon-rose scent and small, lavender flowers. It makes an attractive, good-sized potted plant.

'CANDY DANCER'

The lemon-rose scented leaves are deeply divided and fernlike. Its single lavender flower and habit is similar to that of 'Dr. Livingston', but it is more dense and compact.

Candy Dancer

CAPITATUM (*P. capitatum*)

Plants of this species vary in the strength of the rose fragrance: check the scent before purchasing one. It is sprawling and poorly suited to pots. The single lavender bloom is small and forms dense seed heads, which resenbke tiny hedgehogs.

Crowfoot Rose

'CHARITY'

A sport of an old-fashioned-rose type that has large green incised leaves with a wide, gold edging. This robust plant, with a rose scent overlaid with lemon, is great for the garden or large containers. It has small lavender flowers.

'CROWFOOT ROSE'

The deeply cut leaves have a velvety texture and a scent between rose and lemon-rose. The small lavender flowers are borne in such profusion that they can exhaust the plant; it may be helpful to debud the plant if it looks unhealthy. The outline of the leaf has been likened to the track of a crow's foot, hence the name.

Charity

'DR. LIVINGSTON' ('SKELETON LEAF ROSE')

This tall, rangy plant has deeply cut leaves with a rough, raspy texture and a rose scent. It makes a good background plant in the garden.

Dr. Livingston

Lady Plymouth

Michael Vassar

Michael Vassar

Joe Coca

Rober's Lemon Rose

Old-Fashioned Rose

'LADY PLYMOUTH'

A sport of old-fashioned rose, it has deeply divided, gray-green leaves that are edged and sometimes splotched with white. It has a lovely rose scent and small lavender flowers, and makes a nice potted plant. This variable plant will sport two other named cultivars:

'Grey Lady Plymouth', with a finer white leaf edging, and 'Silver Leaf Rose', which has a silvery cast to the leaf and an even finer white edging than 'Grey Lady Plymouth'.

All three have the same rose scent and flower color, and like 'Lady Plymouth' readily revert to the solid green form, so any green shoots or branches that appear should be removed.

'OLD-FASHIONED ROSE' *(P. graveolens)*

This plant, of medium height, has gray-green, strongly indented leaves, a nice rose scent, and lavender flowers. The most important scented pelargonium for the commercial production of rose-geranium oil, it is also the kind used most often in jams, jellies, and potpourri. It makes an attractive potted plant.

'PEACOCK'

This cultivar is nearly identical to the older 'Both's Snowflake' but usually has whiter stems and petioles and grows more upright. It has a deeply incised leaf with a cream to white hit-or-miss variegation, rose to lemon-rose scent, and small lavender flowers.

'ROBER'S LEMON ROSE'

This is sometimes called the "tomato geranium", because its leaves are irregularly incised and resemble those of a tomato plant. It is a vigorous grower with small lavender flowers and a strong lemon-rose scent.

Michael Vassar

Peacock

'ROUND-LEAF ROSE'

The large, soft, slightly fuzzy leaves of this cultivar have shallow lobes and a good lemon-rose scent. It is sometimes sold as 'Round-Leaf Orange', though it has no orange scent. It is a large and trailing plant with single lavender flowers.

'SNOWFLAKE'

This sport of 'Round-Leaf Rose' has a hit-or-miss white variegation. It is a good cultivar for large hanging baskets. Because it will revert to 'Round-Leaf Rose', all green branches should be removed.

'VARIEGATED GIANT ROSE'

This appears to be a sport of either 'Snowflake' or 'Round-Leaf Rose'. It has gold variegation in a large hit-or-miss pattern and the same lavender flowers, leaf shape and texture, and lemon-rose scent as 'Round-Leaf Rose'.

'VARIEGATED ATTAR OF ROSE'

This recent sport of 'Attar of Rose' is the same in scent and flower. The leaf variegation is creamy gold in a hit-or-miss pattern.

Michael Vassar

Joe Coca

Snowflake

Round-Leaf Rose

Joy Lucille

MINT-SCENTED

Though there are but a few truly mint-scented pelargoniums, their fragrance is often strong and unmistakable. One of them, 'Peppermint' (*P. tomentosum*), is an old-time garden favorite.

Pungent Peppermint

'APPLE MINT'

This cultivar looks like 'Apple' (*P. odoratissimum*), but its scent is both fruity and minty. The soft gray-green leaves are larger than those of the typical apple, as is the entire plant. It has tiny white flowers borne in long sprays and makes a lovely basket plant.

'JOY LUCILLE'

This tall, rangy cultivar is thought to be a cross between *P. graveolens* and *P. tomentosum.* The leaves are more deeply lobed than the latter and have only a light mint scent. The single flowers are pale pink lilac. A sport, 'Variegated Joy Lucille', has a hit-or-miss white variegation.

'MINT-SCENTED ROSE'

This cultivar is similar to 'Lady Plymouth' and has deeply divided gray-green leaves with a cream to white hit-or-miss variegation and border, but its scent is moderately minty. It is sometimes offered as *P. graveolens* 'Variegatum'.

'Peppermint' (*P. tomentosum*)

This large, sprawling plant has large, lobed leaves with a wonderfully soft, velvety texture and sprays of very small white flowers. It can quickly fill up a tub or planter. It is perhaps the mostly strongly scented of the mint-scented varieties. This plant needs more afternoon shade than most scenteds.

'Peppermint Lace'

The leaves of this cultivar are very large, flat, and deeply cut, giving them a lacy look. The texture is velvety, and the scent is strongly minty. The plant is tall and robust and has small, single white flowers.

'Pungent Peppermint' ('Bode's Peppermint')

The leaves of this cultivar are gray-green and deeply cut. They are smaller and have finer lobes than those of ' Peppermint Lace'. The plant is of medium growth and has a nice mint scent and mauve flowers.

'Rollison's Unique'

This robust plant has large curly leaves, a mild mint scent, and single bright magenta flowers.

Mint-Scented Rose

Michael Vassar

Mabel Grey

Michael Vassar

Joe Coca

Citronella

P. Crispum Major

LEMON/CITRUS-SCENTED

This group includes a wide variety of plants, from the tiny-leaved *P. crispum* 'Minor' to the treelike, large-leaved *P. citronellum* ('Mabel Grey'). Many cultivars have a sharp, clean scent and are wonderful in cookery, potpourri, and sachets. Some have been in cultivation for nearly two centuries and are still among the most popular scented pelargoniums.

'CITRONELLA'

This is a large plant with coarse, lobed leaves, a moderate lemon scent, and small lavender flowers. Don't confuse it with the similarly named species *P. citronellum* (see below).

'MABEL GREY' (*P. citronellum*)

Originally introduced as the cultivar 'Mabel Grey', this plant was later determined to be a species and renamed. It has large, sharply lobed rough leaves with a very strong lemon scent. It grows upright and tall, often reaching 6 or 7 feet (2 m) high. The lavender flowers have a darker upper stippling and are fairly large among scenteds. This species is the parent of several cultivars.

P. crispum 'MAJOR'

This cultivar is a large version of *P. crispum* with much larger stems and leaves. It has the same nice, lemon scent and pale lilac flowers.

P. crispum 'MINOR'

This cultivar is similar to *P. crispum*, but has very thin, woody stems. It has the same sweet lemon scent as its larger relative. The custom of floating the minute leaves in finger bowls in Victorian times gave rise to the alternative name 'Fingerbowl Lemon'. Some pelargonium taxonomists believe this to be the original *P. crispum*. The plants may be difficult to root and are not long-lived.

'CRISPUM LATIFOLIUM'

Though this plant bears the crispum name, it differs from the others by having a smoother leaf with only a slightly wavy edge. Its lovely, sweet scent is a combination of lemon, lime, and orange. It can be pruned to an upright shape, or left to cascade from a hanging basket. The pale lilac flowers have a deeper stippling on the upper petal and are larger than those of the true crispums.

P. Crispum Minor

'FRENSHAM' (FRENCHAISE')

The first reported hybrid of *P. citronellum* (the other parent being 'Prince of Orange'), this plant was introduced in England in 1970. The leaves less sharply lobed than *P. citronellum*, and the plant is shorter, but the flowers and scent are the same.

Crispum Latifolium

'LEMONAIRE', 'LEMON FANCY', AND 'LEMON MERINGUE'

These all appear to be *P. citronellum* (Mabel Grey) hybrids and are almost identical to 'Frenscham'. They all have stiff, sharply toothed leaves, a sharp lemon scent, and single, pale lavender flowers.

Joe Coca

Lemonaire

Frenshanm

Galway Star

Hansen's Wild Spice

Ginger

Golden Lemon Crispum

'GALWAY STAR'

This plant resembles 'Variegated Prince Rupert' in leaf and stem but is larger and is blessed with the sharply lemon scent of *P. citronellum*. It has single pale lilac flowers.

'GINGER' ('TORENTO')

This tall, robust plant is similar in appearance to 'Lime' and *crispum* 'Latifolium', but its smooth, round, slightly toothed leaves are larger. The fairly large flowers are lavender with deep purple markings. Some say the scent is of freshly cut ginger, while others detect a citrus overtone.

'GOLDEN LEMON CRISPUM'

A sport of *P. crispum*, this cultivar has green leaves edged with chartreuse and a nice lemon scent.

'HANSEN'S WILD SPICE'

This plant has smooth, slightly toothed leaves and large flowers with rosy pink upper petals and paler pink lower ones. It has a sweet citrus fragrance. If left unpruned, the branches trail, making it a good plant for hanging baskets.

'LADY MARY'

A plant of this name was grown in England during the early 1800s, but it does not match the description of the contemporary 'Lady Mary'. The small, toothed leaves have a faint lemon scent with a rose overtone, and the lovely pure pink flowers have upper petals splotched with reddish rose. Sometimes erroneously sold as 'Strawberry', this cultivar is graceful grown in a hanging basket.

Lady Mary

LEMON (*P. crispum*)

This is the most popular of the lemon-scented pelargoniums. It has small, roundish, crinkled leaves. The stiff stems, if left unpruned, cascade as they lengthen, making this an attractive basket plant.

Lemon

'LEMON BALM'

This large, very tall plant has coarse, lobed leaves and a pungent lemon scent. It has small, single lavender flowers.

'LIME'

The roundish leaves are smooth, slightly ruffled, and sweetly lime-scented. The flowers, larger than most, are pale lavender with deep purple spots on the upper petals. The plant will grow tall and lanky if not pruned frequently. This cultivar is not a true species but is sometimes listed incorrectly with the Latin species epithet of *nervosum.* 'Dorcas Brigham Lime', a sport selected by its namesake, is a larger plant with a slightly stronger scent.

Lime

Lemon Balm

'LIMONEUM'

Another cultivar with a species-sounding name. The small, saw-toothed leaves have a sweet lemon-lime fragrance, and the flowers are a deep rose purple. Thin, lax stems make this a good plant for hanging baskets. The plant is sometimes erroneously sold as 'Cinnamon'.

Michael Vassar

Orange

'ORANGE'

This plant has large, saw-toothed leaves with a sweet orange scent and is of a medium, upright growth. The large single flowers are very pale lilac with deep purple splotches on the upper petals. This is often erroneously listed as 'Prince of Orange', which is a different cultivar.

'PRINCE OF ORANGE'

This plant has been cultivated in England since the 1800s. It has small, serrated leaves with a mild mandarin orange scent. The flowers are pale lavender with a small darker purple spot on the upper petals. This plant is rarely seen or offered for sale in the United States, and is smaller in stature than 'Orange'.

'PRINCE RUPERT'

This plant is similar to *P. crispum,* but the leaves are slightly lobed, and the scent is neither as sweet nor as strong.

'Variegated Prince Rupert', which is sometimes listed as 'French Lace' or *P. crispum* 'Variegatum', has leaves edged with cream and white and a fainter scent than 'Prince Rupert'.

'ROGER'S DELIGHT'

This regal pelargonium is a large, floppy plant with a nice lemon scent. The large flowers have reddish purple upper petals and paler lavender-rose lower petals. It is suitable for hanging baskets.

Upright Coconut (*P. elongatum*)

This plant has a round, serrated leaf with a distinct dark brown zone and a mild citrus scent despite its name. It is a floppy plant, suitable for hanging baskets, with small flowers of pale, creamy yellow. It is sometimes incorrectly listed as *P. patulum,* which is a different species with a pink flower.

Upright Coconut

Fringed Apple

Joe Coca

Concolor Lace

Fruit and Nut-Scented

Though most of the members of this group are sweetly scented, their names in many cases do not accurately describe their fragrances. Don't be surprised if you don't detect the scent that the name suggests.

'Almond' ('Pretty Polly')

The deeply lobed leaves of this cultivar develop a slightly brownish center when grown in strong sunlight. The flowers are bright pink with rosy red spots on the upper petals. Some liken the scent to that of almond leaves while others find it slightly pungent.

'Apple' (*P. odoratissimum*)

This species has soft, gray-green leaves and a refreshing apple-cider scent. It grows in a low clump, and its tiny white flowers are produced on long trailing sprays. It looks great in a hanging basket.

Joe Coca

Almond

'Coconut' (*P. grossularioides*)

The leaves of this species are small, round, and deep green. It forms a low-growing mound of foliage with long sprays of very small magenta flowers. It has a pleasant scent, though not necessarily that of coconut, and self-seeds freely.

'Concolor Lace' ('Filbert', 'Shottesham Pet')

The light green, deeply divided leaves of this cultivar somewhat resemble carrot leaves and are supposed to smell like filbert leaves but are actually only faintly pungent. A pretty plant, with small, bright red flowers, that is handsome in pots.

Joe Coca

Coconut

Paton's Unique

'FRINGED APPLE'

Similar to 'Apple', of which it was a seedling, the leaves have a fringed, serrated edge, and the scent is a bit more pungent.

'PATON'S UNIQUE' ('APRICOT')

This cultivar is best known in the United States as 'Apricot', though the correct name dates back to its introduction in England in 1870. It has deeply lobed, dark green leaves, with a pungent scent. The lovely flowers are larger than those of most other scenteds, are rounded, and have pink and rose petals punctuated by a small, white eye. The cultivar has several named sports:

'Madame Nonin' has a flower with wider, frilly petals that appears doubled. The leaves have the same scent as 'Paton's Unique' but are more serrated. It will readily revert to 'Paton's Unique'.

'Mexican Sage' ('Light Pink Paton's Unique') is identical in form and scent to 'Paton's Unique', but the flower is a very pale pink lilac. The sport reverts back to the regular flower readily, and sometimes both flower colors can be found on the same plant.

Peach

'PHYLLIS'

The flowers' scent and growth pattern are the same as those of 'Paton's Unique', but the leaves have a wide white border.

'PEACH' ('GOOSEBERRY-LEAF')

The roundish leaves are small, have 'crisped' edges, and are variegated with cream or white in a hit-or-miss pattern. The thin stems tend to bend downward if left unpruned. The scent is faintly citrus, and the single flowers are very pale lilac.

'STRAWBERRY' ('COUNTESS OF SCARBOROUGH')

This cultivar has small, dark green trilobed leaves with a crinkled edge and the sweet fragrance of strawberry and citrus. The flowers are pale pink with darker markings on the upper petals. Thin-stemmed and lax, 'Strawberry' makes a nice basket subject.

Brunswick

Aroma

PUNGENT-SCENTED

These are the scented pelargoniums that don't quite fit into the other categories. In some cultivars, the fragrance is strong, while in others it is very faint. A few are virtually scentless and are best grown for their flowers. While most people find the rose, mint, and lemon/ citrus fragrances pleasing, some people do not enjoy the pungent scenteds. Included here are the "oaks", a vague group most of whose members have softly lobed leaves shaped like oak leaves.

'AROMA'

The small round gray-green leaves of this cultivar are curly and smell like those of 'Nutmeg' but are less pungent. It is a low, dense clumping plant with tiny white flowers on trailing sprays, making it a good choice for hanging baskets.

'BRILLIANT'

This cultivar has lobed leaves with a medium pungent scent. The single flowers are cerise purple. Sometimes erronesouly listed as 'California Brilliant', it sports a plant with pale lavender flowers, 'Sonoma Lavender'.

'BRUNSWICK'

The large leaves of this large, sprawling cultivar have a slightly pungent scent. It is worth growing for the showy, deep rose flowers with dark stippling.

Chocolate Mint

'CHOCOLATE MINT'

This hybrid of 'Peppermint' and 'Giant Oak' has leaves shaped like those of the latter, but they lack the peppermint scent and wonderful fuzziness. The name "chocolate" refers to the attractive, brownish purple blotch in the center of each leaf, not to the scent, which is pungent. It has small lavender flowers.

'CLORINDA'

This big, rangy plant has shallowly lobed leaves and a scent that has been described variously as eucalyptus, cedar, or pleasantly pungent. It is usually grown for its large, bright pink flowers. 'Golden Clorinda' is a sport which is identical to its parent except for gold-edged leaves.

'COPTHORNE'

This very tall, rangy plant has large, trilobed leaves and is considered by some to smell of cedar and by others to be merely pungent. Its pale lavender flowers are larger than those of most other scenteds and bloom over a longer period.

Michael Vassar

Dean's Delight

'DEAN'S DELIGHT'

This low-growing cultivar has deeply cut, dark green leaves and a strongly pungent scent. The two upper petals of the pale lavender flowers are split down the middle, making them appear to have four upper petals. The plant is very attractive in containers.

Michael Vassar

Clorinda

P. dichondrifolium

This low, compact species has roundish, gray-green leaves and trailing stems of small white flowers. The pungent scent is of freshly ground pepper.

Michael Vassar

P. dichondrifolium

Michael Vassar

Copthorne

Fair Ellen

'FAIR ELLEN'

The leaves are large and shallowly lobed with purple-brown midrib markings. They are somewhat sticky and have a strong pungent scent. The flowers are lavender with dark stippling. This is one of the lower-growing oak types and looks good in pots.

'FERN-LEAF' (*P. denticulatum*)

The leaves of this tall-growing species are dark green, sticky, and very finely cut. They are considered by some to smell of pine while others call it merely pungent. The flowers are small and lavender. It is sometimes listed as 'Filicifolium'.

Lillian Pottinger

GRAPE-LEAF (*P. hispidum*)

The large, rough leaves of this species are shaped like grape leaves and are moderately pungent. The upper petals of the pale lilac flowers are much larger than the lower ones. A very large plant, it can grow more than 7 feet (2 m) tall. Grape-leaf is sometimes erroneously listed as *P. vitifolium* because the species epithet means "grape leaf" in Latin. *P. vitifolium*, however, is decidedly rose scented.

'JUNIPER'

This hybrid, reported as a chance seedling from *P. crispum*, looks very similar to *P. crispum*, with small, round, crinkled leaves, but the leaves have the fragrance of juniper foliage. It has single, very pale lilac flowers.

'LILIAN POTTINGER'

The small, camphor-scented gray-green leaves of this cultivar have a fringed edge, giving them a lacy appearance. A compact plant, with sprays of tiny white flowers, it looks very handsome in baskets.

Grape-Leaf

'LITTLE GEM'

This cultivar is often erroneously listed as being rose-scented, perhaps because its leaves resemble those of 'Old-Fashioned Rose', but the fragrance is mildly pungent. The plant is of compact growth, medium height, and has small lavender flowers.

'MRS. KINGSLEY' ('MRS. KINGSBURY')

This is a large, semi-trailing plant with curly, gray-green leaves and a slightly pungent scent. It is grown mainly for its single, bright cerise flowers.

'MRS. TAYLOR'

This large, sprawling plant has deeply cut, crinkly, slightly scented leaves. Its attractive flowers are bright red with nearly black markings on the upper petals.

'NUTMEG'

This plant is similar to 'Apple', with small, round gray-green leaves and white flowers, but the scent is strongly pungent and spicy, said by some to resemble that of fresh nutmeg. The growth is dense and clumped. It has sported several variegated forms, which all look good in baskets.

'Golden Nutmeg' has grayish leaves with a yellow border.

'Snowy Nutmeg' has variegation in pure white.

'Variegated Nutmeg' has a hit-or-miss cream to white pattern. All three cultivars readily revert back to green or sport variegations similar to those of the other types. Careful pruning and propagation is necessary to maintain the cultivars.

Michael Vassar

Little Gem

Michael Vassar

Mrs. Kingsley

Michael Vassar

Snowy Nutmeg

Red-Flowered Rose

'OLD SPICE'

This cultivar is similar to nutmeg, but its scent is more pungent and less spicy.

'POQUITO'

The rough, somewhat sticky leaves of this cultivar are deeply divided with purple-brown midribs. The scent is strongly pungent. The flowers are lavender with darker stippling. The plant is low and bushy and makes a pretty display in containers.

'PHEASANT'S FOOT'

Similar to fern-leaf and thought to be another form of *P. denticulatum*, the sticky leaves are less finely divided and have broader ribs. It has a pungent scent. The flowers are single and lavender.

Pheasant's Foot

'RED-FLOWERED ROSE'

The leaves of this tall, rangy plant are dark green and deeply lobed with a wavy edge. They bear a resemblance to those of 'Old-Fashioned Rose', hence the name, but the scent is merely pungent. Grow it for its flowers which are bright red, with deeper coloration on the upper petals.

'SHRUBLAND ROSE'

This is another cultivar which misleadingly has "rose" in its name but whose scent is pungent. It is a large plant, 2 to 3 feet (1/2 to 1 meter) tall, with glossy, dark green leaves and bright red flowers.

Shrubland Rose

'SOUTHERNWOOD' (*P. abrotanifolium*)

The small, gray-green leaves of this species are narrowly divided and have a scent similar to the herb southernwood (*Artemisia abrotanum*). The small flowers are usually white, but purple-flowered cultivars are also available, and the long stems are generally trailing. There is also a dwarf, compact purple-flowered form.

'Sweet Miriam' ('Sweet Mimosa')

Often reported to have a sweet rose scent, this robust, large, and sprawling cultivar has moderately pungent, deeply cut leaves and pretty, pure pink flowers.

'Variegated Oak Leaf'

The leaves of this large, sprawling cultivar are large, coarse, and pungently scented. The variegation is a hit-or-miss pattern of cream to white. The lavender flowers are fairly large, and the plant blooms more freely than most other oak types.

'Village Hill Oak'

The attractive, strongly pungent leaves of this plant are deeply divided with a very curly edge. The flowers are lavender.

Joe Coca

Village Hill Oak

Joe Coca

Variegated Oak Leaf

ANNOTATED BIBLIOGRAPHY

Bailey, L.H. *How Plants Get Their Names*. New York: Dover Publications, 1963. An entertaining look at botanical nomenclature including a pronunciation guide and dictionary of specific epithets.

Clark, David. *Pelargoniums*. Portland, OR: Timber Press, 1988. Part of the "Kew Gardening Series", it is a general look at pelargoniums and their cultivation.

Condor, Susan. *The Complete Geranium*. New York: Clarkson Potter, 1992. Contains a useful section of recipes featuring scenteds.

Stearn, William. *Dictionary of Plant Names for Gardeners*. London: Cassell Publishers, 1992. A thorough dictionary for the derivations of generic and specific names.

White, John, editor. *Geraniums IV*. Geneva, IL: Ball Publishing, 1993. A compendium of articles, many technical, focusing on commercial pelargonium production.

Wilson, Helen Van Pelt. *The Joy of Geraniums*. New York: M. Barrows & Co., 1965. A wonderful guide covering all types of pelargoniums. First published in 1946, this classic text went through several editions. Now out of print, it can still be found in libraries and used bookstores.

You can also find small sections about scented pelargoniums in many herb books. Look for more recipes in cookbooks that feature herbs, particularly in the writings of Adelma Simmons.

SOURCES

SEEDS AND PLANTS

Deerwood Geraniums
Rt 4, Box 525A
Buckhannon, WV 26201
Phone (304) 472-4203
Catalog $3

Geraniaceae
122 Hillcrest Ave.
Kentfield, CA 94094
Phone/Fax (415) 461-4168
By appointment only

Goodwin Creek Gardens
PO Box 83
Williams, OR 97544
Phone/Fax (541) 846-7357
Catalog $1

Logee's Greenhouses
141 North St.
Danielson, CT 06239
Catalog $3

Rasland Farm
NC 82 at US 12
Godwin, NC 28344
Catalog $3

Richter's
357 Highway 47
Goodwood, Ontario L0C 1A0 Canada
Phone (905) 640-6677
Catalog free

Well-Sweep Herb Farm
205 Mt. Bethel Rd.
Port Murray, NJ 07865
Phone (908) 852-5390
Catalog $2

SUPPLIES

A.M. Leonard, Inc.
241 Fox Dr., PO Box 816,
Piqua, OH 45356
Great source of tools and instruments including pH meters and heating mats.

Gardener's Supply Company
128 Intervale Rd.
Burlington, VT 05401
Tools and pesticides for the home gardener.

Peaceful Valley Farm Supply
PO Box 2209
Grass Valley, CA 95945
Large selection of organic pesticides as well as tools.

ASSOCIATIONS

International Geranium Society
PO Box 92734
Pasadena, CA 91109
This society promotes the understanding and cultivation of the geranium family, including all types of pelargoniums. Yearly membership dues ($12.50) include a quarterly newsletter, a sample of which can also be obtained for $3.

INDEX

*Page numbers in bold
indicate main entry
in the varieties section.*